Welcome to
South America!

Jill McDougall

Welcome to South America!

Text: Jill McDougall
Publishers: Tania Mazzeo and Eliza Webb
Series consultant: Amanda Sutera
  Hands on Heads Consulting
Editor: Sarah Layton
Project editor: Annabel Smith
Designer: Leigh Ashforth
Project designer: Danielle Maccarone
Illustrations and maps: Dave Smith
Permissions researcher: Helen Mammides
Production controller: Renee Tome

Acknowledgements
We would like to thank the following for permission to reproduce
copyright material:

Front cover: iStock.com/shalamov; pp. 1, 19 (top): Getty Images/
Thomas Janisch; p. 5 (top): Shutterstock.com/R.M. Nunes, (bottom):
Shutterstock.com/reptiles4all; p. 6: Shutterstock.com/worldclassphoto;
p. 7 (top left): Alamy Stock Photo/Hemis, (top middle): iStock.com/
Grafissimo, (top right): Alamy Stock Photo/dimkaru/Stockimo, (bottom):
Alamy Stock Photo/Francisco de Casa; p. 8 (main): Nature Picture
Library/Karine Aigner, (inset): Alamy Stock Photo/RGB Ventures/
SuperStock; p. 9: Shutterstock.com/PARALAXIS; p. 10, back cover:
Shutterstock.com/saiko3p; p. 11 (main): iStock.com/juliandoporai,
(inset): Shutterstock.com/Milton Rodriguez; p. 13 (top): Alamy Stock
Photo/Lordprice Collection, (middle): Alamy Stock Photo/Pictorial Press
Ltd; p. 14: Shutterstock.com/tomowen; pp. 15 (main), 24: Shutterstock.
com/FOTOGRIN; p. 15 (inset): iStock.com/4FR; p. 16 (main): Shutterstock.
com/NaturesMomentsuk, (inset): Shutterstock.com/Tomas Kotouc;
p. 17 (left): iStock.com/elmvilla, (right): Shutterstock.com/Don Mammoser,
(inset): Alamy Stock Photo/KGPA Ltd; p. 18: Alamy Stock Photo/Karol
Kozlowski Premium RM Collection; p. 19 (middle): Alamy Stock
Photo/Premaphotos, (bottom): Age Fotostock/Zoonar.com/Julian Peters;
p. 21 (main): Alamy Stock Photo/Minden Pictures, (inset): Alamy Stock
Photo/Hanjo Hellmann; p. 22: iStock.com/noblige.

Every effort has been made to trace and acknowledge copyright.
However, if any infringement has occurred, the publishers tender their
apologies and invite the copyright holders to contact them.

NovaStar

Text © 2024 Cengage Learning Australia Pty Limited
Illustrations © 2024 Cengage Learning Australia Pty Limited

ISBN 978 0 17 033426 6

Cengage Learning Australia
Level 5, 80 Dorcas Street
Southbank VIC 3006 Australia
Phone: 1300 790 853
Email: aust.nelsonprimary@cengage.com

For learning solutions, visit **cengage.com.au**

Printed in China by 1010 Printing International Ltd
1 2 3 4 5 6 7 28 27 26 25 24

*Nelson acknowledges the Traditional Owners and Custodians
of the lands of all First Nations Peoples. We pay respect
to Elders past and present, and extend that respect to
all First Nations Peoples today.*

Contents

A Land of Extremes

Welcome to South America! If you check out the map, you'll see that South America lies in the **Western Hemisphere** of Earth. This large continent is made up of 12 countries. It stretches north from just above the **equator** and south towards the icy Antarctic.

A Map of South America

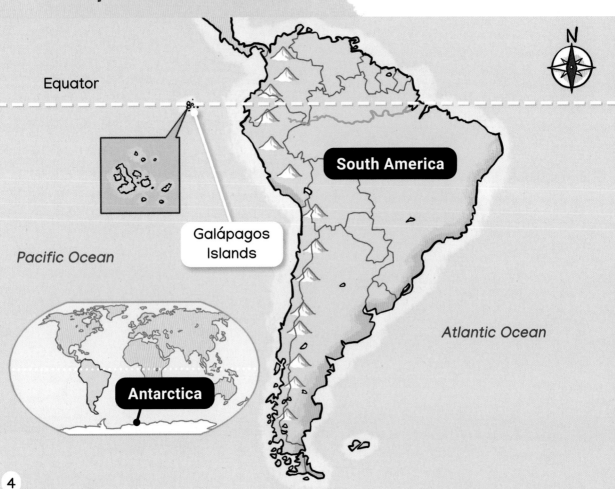

Equator

Galápagos Islands

Pacific Ocean

South America

Antarctica

Atlantic Ocean

N

It is fair to say that South America is a land of extremes. It has *extremely* large forests and rivers, an *extremely* dry desert and an *extremely* long mountain range. In fact, South America holds several world-beating records.

Iguazu Falls, Argentina, South America

South America's Hall of Fame

World record for ...	And it goes to ...	Size
largest rainforest	the Amazon Rainforest	over 6 million square kilometres
longest mountain range	the Andes (say: *an–deez*) Mountains	8900 kilometres long
tallest waterfall	Angel Falls	979 metres high
longest country	Chile	4300 kilometres long

And if that isn't enough, South America is home to the world's most poisonous frog, the poison dart frog!

So, pack your camera and hiking boots and get ready to explore this unique place.

poison dart frog

The Amazon Rainforest

The Amazon Rainforest covers 40 per cent of South America and is spread across nine countries. It's named after the Amazon River, which starts in the Andes Mountains and winds through the rainforest to the ocean.

Are you ready to take a look? Don't forget your waterproof jacket! After all, we are in a *rain*forest.

N

Amazon River

Andes Mountains

Atlantic Ocean

Key:

Amazon Rainforest

At its widest point, the Amazon River is 11 kilometres from one side to the other.

red-faced spider monkey

giant toucan

blue morpho butterflies

You might notice the air here is warm and moist, and you're surrounded by thick jungle. That's because we are in the **tropics**, and a tropical **climate** is perfect for many different trees, vines and ferns. Look up and you'll see that leafy plants have formed a green **canopy** overhead. Up there, in the sunlight, flowers and fruit **thrive**. In fact, they provide a non-stop picnic for rainforest animals like monkeys, tropical birds and giant butterflies.

Listen! All around you are the sounds of humming, buzzing and chirping. The rainforest is **teeming** with millions of animals and insects. There are so many that scientists are discovering new ones every day.

Plants as Medicine

Many medicines used around the world come from plants found only in the Amazon Rainforest.

Wasai root can be ground up and taken as tea to stay in good health.

Tread quietly through the jungle and you might spot a giant anteater in the undergrowth or a red-eyed tree frog clinging to a leaf. You might even glimpse a jaguar moving silently through the trees or a shy tapir eating fallen fruit.

tapir

The Amazon Rainforest supports a delicate web of life that includes plants, mammals, reptiles, birds and insects. Many plants and animals have formed relationships that benefit one another. The trees benefit birds and animals by providing fruit for them to eat. When they eat the fruit, the birds and animals benefit the trees by spreading their seeds to new parts of the forest, often in their droppings. This kind of helpful partnership is called **symbiosis** (say: *sim-by-oh-sis*).

A jaguar wades through water in the Amazon Rainforest.

You'd think that such a special place would be carefully protected, wouldn't you? Think again. The Amazon Rainforest is under threat as more and more trees are cut down by farmers and mining companies. However, many **Indigenous peoples** who live here are working with **conservation groups** to help save the rainforest.

Large areas of the Amazon Rainforest have been cleared by burning land and cutting down trees.

The Shrinking Amazon Rainforest

Why is it shrinking?	What is the result?
Causes	Effects
* Logs are taken to make paper, furniture and houses. * Land is cleared to grow crops and build roads and mines.	* Indigenous peoples lose their homes, traditional food and medicine. * Animals and plants lose their habitats.

Machu Picchu

A visit to Machu Picchu (say: *match-oo pi-choo*) in Peru will give you a sense of some of the history of South America. It's a place of mysterious city **ruins** that sit high in the Andes Mountains.

Machu Picchu means "old mountain" in the local language. It was built by the people of the Inca **empire** in the 15th century – over 600 years ago!

Machu Picchu sits at the top of a mountain in Peru.

Where Is Machu Pic–chu?

N

Amazon River

PERU

Andes Mountains

Atlantic Ocean

Key:

● Machu Picchu

The Inca were expert builders who **constructed** more than 200 buildings on the Machu Picchu site, including a royal palace. One important building is known as the Temple of the Sun. The walls are made of polished stones, fitted closely together. Twice a year, sunlight shines through the windows onto a special stone inside the temple. The temple may have been built as a place to **worship** a sun god.

the Temple of the Sun, Machu Picchu

Furry Helpers

The llama was an important animal to the Inca people. Llamas provided wool and food, and they could carry heavy loads. Llamas are still used by locals today!

11

Why Did People Leave Machu Picchu?

One hundred years after Machu Picchu was built, it was suddenly abandoned. Why did everyone leave? Historians aren't certain, but here is one popular idea.

Machu Picchu may have been built as a royal estate – a luxurious home for the Inca emperor Pachacuti (say: *patch-a-koo-tee*).

Then, in 1532, Spanish fighters invaded the Inca empire. The Incas fought back with arrows and spears, but the Spanish army had swords and guns (known as muskets). The invaders also brought diseases like smallpox and measles that killed many Inca fighters.

By 1572, the Spanish invaders had defeated the Inca empire and gained control of the land. This meant that there were no further Inca emperors to occupy the royal estate and, as a result, it slowly turned into ruins.

The Spanish invaders lived in the valleys below Machu Picchu, but they never found this secret place hidden high in the mountains. It wasn't until 1911 that an American man named Hiram Bingham III climbed to the top of a mountain and discovered the ruins.

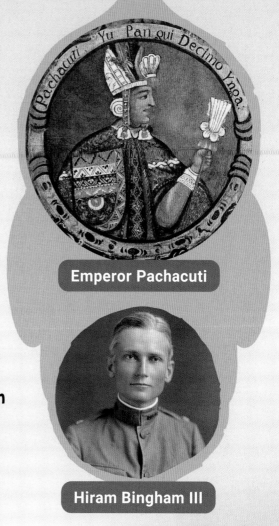

Emperor Pachacuti

Hiram Bingham III

the Inca at Machu Picchu

Galápagos Islands

The Galápagos Islands lie in the Pacific Ocean, about 1000 kilometres from the coast of Ecuador. The islands were formed by fierce volcanoes that erupted under the ocean millions of years ago. When the volcanoes rose above the sea, they gradually became a group of islands.

Here, you can walk across the **lava fields** with their swirling black patterns and imagine that everything under your feet once came from inside a volcano.

Where Are the Galápagos Islands?

ECUADOR

N

Amazon River

Pacific Ocean

Andes Mountains

Key:

Galápagos Islands

The patterns on the rock were made when the lava first dried.

The Galápagos Islands are home to many **species** of rare wildlife. In fact, some creatures cannot be found anywhere else in the world. How did they get here? By swimming, floating or flying!

The Galápagos tortoise is a large reptile that floated from the South American coast to the islands millions of years ago. These gigantic creatures are the largest tortoises on the planet, weighing up to 300 kilograms. That's as heavy as your average-sized grizzly bear!

Galápagos tortoises can live for more than 100 years!

What's in a Name?

The Galápagos Islands were named after the giant tortoise – *galápago* is the Spanish word for tortoise.

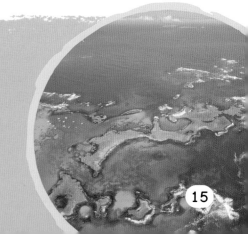

As you stroll along the rocky shore, you might notice large lizards basking in the sun. These are marine iguanas (say: *ig-wah-nez*), and they are the only lizards on Earth that spend time in the ocean. You may spot them snorting out water and think: *what an odd habit!* Well, you see, the **algae** that marine iguanas eat in the ocean is very salty, so they need to "sneeze" to remove the extra salt from their bodies.

Eleven types of marine iguanas live on the Galápagos Islands.

You'll probably want your camera ready when you spot the brightly coloured crabs crawling over the black lava rocks. These are Sally Lightfoot crabs that feed on **debris** washed in from the ocean. You might even see them picking bugs off a sleeping marine iguana with their claws!

Sally Lightfoot crab

Do you hear that loud bark? That's a sea lion on the beach, guarding his area. And that hoarse quacking sound? That's a bird called the blue-footed booby that really does have blue feet!

sea lion

blue-footed booby

The Galápagos Islands are full of surprises. It's no wonder this unique part of the world is a **World Heritage site**.

 ## Charles Darwin

In 1835, a young scientist named Charles Darwin visited the Galápagos Islands. He realised that the animals on the islands had evolved, or changed over time, to suit the environment. Darwin's idea is called "evolution".

Charles Darwin, 1890

The Atacama Desert

The Atacama Desert is a long, narrow desert that stretches down the coast of Chile between the Pacific Ocean and the Andes Mountains. This rocky landscape is the driest desert on Earth. In fact, it hardly ever rains in the Atacama Desert. How could animals and plants survive here?

Let's take a closer look ...

There are places in the Atacama Desert that haven't had rain in over 500 years.

Where Is the Atacama Desert?

N

Amazon River

Andes Mountains

CHILE

Atlantic Ocean

Key:

Atacama Desert

Animals that live in the Atacama Desert have adapted to the harsh environment in different ways. The vicuña (say: *vuh-koo-nyah*) is a woolly mammal that feeds on spiky desert plants. It has a tough mouth that can deal with the sharpest thorns!

vicuña

The tiny leaf-eared mouse also survives in the dusty desert. It hunts for small seeds and fruits that contain enough moisture for its survival.

leaf-eared mouse

You might be surprised to see shallow lakes in the dry landscape. The salty water slowly flows up from underground. The water was trapped there millions of years ago. Flocks of long-legged flamingos wade in the water, feeding on algae.

The flamingos get their pink colour from eating the red algae that grows in the salt lakes.

Water is the key to survival for plants in the Atacama Desert. Water is precious here, and desert plants have a variety of ways to soak up and preserve every last drop.

How do different plants do this?

Do they …

A store water in thick, fleshy leaves?

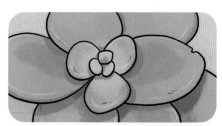

B grow needle-like leaves that prevent water from escaping?

C have a waxy coating on their leaves to trap water inside?

D have extra-long roots to draw moisture from the soil?

E all of the above

If you said "E", congratulations. You're a desert plant expert!

Let's take a closer look at the cactus.
But not too close – those spines
can be sharp!

The cactus plant is well suited to
a desert climate, and it can survive
for years on very little water.

The spines on cactuses keep animals
away and protect the moisture inside.

Many plants in the Atacama Desert
survive on moisture from fog that
rolls in from the Pacific Ocean.

Why Is the Atacama Desert so Dry?

The Andes Mountains act like a giant wall that blocks
rain-carrying clouds from reaching the Atacama Desert.
This means the desert is in a rain shadow.

Our Adventure Ends

Phew! South America is indeed a land of extremes. We've strolled through a steamy rainforest, explored ancient ruins, wandered over volcanic islands with rare wildlife and visited one of the driest deserts in the world!

Our adventure has taken us to many unique environments that deserve special protection and care. There's much more to see, but for now, it's time to say farewell to this amazing continent.

Glossary

algae (*noun*) — simple plants like seaweed that grow in or near water

canopy (*noun*) — the upper layer of tree branches in a forest

climate (*noun*) — weather patterns throughout the year

conservation groups (*noun*) — people who work together to save and protect the environment

constructed (*verb*) — when something is built or made

debris (*noun*) — rubbish or leftover pieces of something broken

emperor (*noun*) — the male ruler of an empire

empire (*noun*) — a group of countries controlled by a single ruler

equator (*noun*) — an imaginary line around the middle of Earth, dividing it into two equal halves

Indigenous peoples (*noun*) — the first peoples living in an area

lava fields (*noun*) — hardened basalt rock that forms after a volcano erupts

rain shadow (*noun*) — an area that has little rainfall because it is sheltered by mountains

ruins (*noun*) — old buildings that are partly destroyed

species (*noun*) — types of animals or plants

symbiosis (*noun*) — when creatures that live nearby help each other

teeming (*adjective*) — full of people or animals moving around

thrive (*verb*) — to be successful and healthy

tropics (*noun*) — hot, often rainy and humid places close to the equator

Western Hemisphere (*noun*) — the western half of planet Earth

World Heritage site (*noun*) — a place of great importance that is given special protection

worship (*verb*) — to show respect for a god

Index